WONDER VERSE

Moonbeam Dreams

First published in Great Britain in 2025 by:

Young Writers
Remus House
Coltsfoot Drive
Peterborough
PE2 9BF
Telephone: 01733 890066
Website: www.youngwriters.co.uk

Book Design by Neila Cepulionyte

Softback ISBN 978-1-83685-442-5
Printed and bound in the UK by BookPrintingUK
Website: www.bookprintinguk.com
YB0638CZ

FOREWORD

WELCOME READER,

For Young Writers' latest competition *Wonderverse*, we asked primary school pupils to explore their creativity and write a poem on any topic that inspired them. They rose to the challenge magnificently with some going even further and writing stories too! The result is this fantastic collection of writing in a variety of styles.

Here at Young Writers our aim is to encourage creativity in children and to inspire a love of the written word, so it's great to get such an amazing response, with some absolutely fantastic pieces. This open theme of this competition allowed them to write freely about something they are interested in, which we know helps to engage kids and get them writing. Within these pages you'll find a variety of topics, from hopes, fears and dreams, to favourite things and worlds of imagination. The result is a collection of brilliant writing that showcases the creativity and writing ability of the next generation.

I'd like to congratulate all the young writers in this anthology, I hope this inspires them to continue with their creative writing.

CONTENTS

Isabelle Baddick (8) 141
Nancy Smith (8) 142
Thomas Barnes (8) 143
Emily Hamlet (9) 144

Sonning CE Primary School, Sonning

Florence Biddulph (9) 145
Emilia Belk (8) 146
Evie Harmston (8) 147
Tilly Bigus (8) 148
Minahil Ayaz (8) 149
Ashling Hyland (9) 150
Lilliana-Rose Bastin (8) 151
Gianveer Sangatpreet Singh Sidhu (8) 152
Abbey Redfern (8) 153
Izzy Sawyer (8) 154
Raife Wilkes (9) 155
Minahil Lone (9) 156

St Bernadette RC Junior School, Clapham Park

Chizoba E Opurum (10) 157
Pawel Kuras (9) 158
Milan M (10) 160
Jeffrey B (9) 162
Remiel Reid (10) 163
Welwitschia (10) 164
Lucciana Q (9) 165
Soraiya C (10) 166
Mirabelle R (10) 167
Hanna G (10) 168
Sharon Munoz Serna (9) 169
Leonardo Marin (9) 170
Hillary A B Otieno (9) 171
Sanchez Blake (9) 172
Godswill O (9) 173
Silva M (9) 174
Sofia Oliveira (10) 175
Zosia K (9) 176
Noah M (10) 177
Emma Figueira de Jesus (9) 178
Anastasia A (10) 179
Matilde Alves 180

St Patrick's Primary School, Coalisland

Holly McCann (9) 181
Lily Quinn (9) 182
Ara McCann (9) 183
Daniel Harte (8) 184
Aoibhe Toner (8) 186
Evie-Grace Gates (9) 187
Pearse O'Neill (10) 188
Eabha Hughes (11) 189
Daire Kilpatrick (9) 190
Cathaoir McKee (9) 191
Logan O'neill (11) 192
Mollie Dorman (10) 193
Niamh Hughes (9) 194
Rhys Conlan (9) 195
Oisín O'Neill (9) 196
Grace Coyle (10) 197
Maia McKee (10) 198
Alfie McClure (9) 199
Tom McAtaseney (9) 200
Eva Coyle (8) 201
Tom Brady (9) 202
Peter Boyle (9) 203
Niamh Quinn (9) 204

THE POEMS
AND
STORIES
GO
1035

Dinosaurs!

D inosaurs ruled our wonderful world once, long
before us. Here are a few and how it ended.
I guanodon hooks leaves on its thumb claw,
devouring them like a lion eats meat.
N igersaurus is a giant, balancing on its hind legs to
reach the juiciest leaves.
O stagrikosaurus prowls through the jungle, fearlessly
hunting its terrified prey like a hawk.
S pinosaurus is a menace, rocketing down rivers as it
catches fish in its inescapable jaws.
A nkylosaurus swings its tail like a mace at any would-
be predator
U tahraptor, who is a ferocious fiend, dashes through
the field with its gleaming claws.
R aptors, as fast as Usain Bolt, dart after their
petrified prey.
S mash! A menacing meteorite crashes into the Earth.
Ending the era of dinosaurs.

Harris Burton (10)
Altrincham Preparatory School, Altrincham

The Void

In the vault of endless night,
The silver wanderer streaks its flight,
A frost-streaked sky, the world's breath stilled,
A darkened sea where stars are spilled.

The fire serpent, it its endless chase,
Spins the web of time in vast embrace,
Where sky-shepherds guide the ship of light,
And moon's tear is swallowed by the void's bite.

The iron heart, a fiery forge,
Sings of creation at the cosmic gorge,
A dream thread woven, winding through,
In the loom of the deep, both old and new.

The sun's forge is the sea of dawn,
While Earth's pulse is the shadow it spawns,
In the whale-road, a ship of the night,
Its prow cuts through the blackened light.

O, the raven's cloak of velvet dark,
Veils the mystery of he light's spark,
Where space's heart, the endless frost,
Drifts in silence, lost but not lost.

Through the blackness, the starship flies,
The winds of time where silence dies,
A fire-bridge arcing 'cross the skies,
In the cold, a flame that never lies.

Aayan Eissa Owais (11)
Altrincham Preparatory School, Altrincham

Winter's Snowy Scenes

The round, pearl-like moon
Shone onto the crisp, white snow,
Transforming the ground into a million stars.

The evergreen trees stood strong
And tall, braving the relentless
Attacks of unforgiving hail.

Icicles dangled from the rough roof
Of hidden caves - chandeliers of Earth's creation.

The soft, silky snow fluttered
Down from the vast sky, casting
Everything in a shiny white.

The wonderful winter scene
Is a feast for the eyes.
You'll know that winter's begun
When the first snowflakes fly.

Yifan Wang (11)
Altrincham Preparatory School, Altrincham

The Life Of Hania Uryszek

When I was born, I was struck with a roar!
Every time I giggled, I started to wiggle
Then I turned one, I had some fun
I learnt to walk, I learnt to talk
Then the age two appeared, oh my, I was a nightmare
Everywhere I went, I made a mess
Anywhere I stayed, there was a mess
Then at three, I had some emotional times
Time flies by in the sky
Sad times fly by through the brain
Then at four, I put my eyes on a sport
Kick and punch, there I came
White and black there I went
Then at five, I learnt to fight
I learnt to write
Then six appeared, I learnt to do a backward roll
I learnt to do a forward roll
By the time I was seven, I learnt to wash
I learnt to cook
At the age of eight, I learnt to draw
I learnt to roar louder
At the age of nine, I learnt to multiply and divide.

Hania Uryszek (9)
Boothferry Primary School, Goole

The Silly Astronaut

I am Tilly,
Who really likes chilli,
I fly to the moon,
Maybe it is my doom,
I place my party hat on,
And twist my nose, which I already have on,
I jump on Mercury,
And I jump on Venus,
And jump on the moon,
It looks like an empty grey room,
Then I go to Mars,
So I jump on Jupiter,
And I jump on Saturn,
And I think it is a lantern,
But I realise it is a satellite,
So I jump on Uranus,
And so I jump onto Neptune,
And the wind has torn me into pieces,
I know it is my doom.

Polina Zdanovska
Boothferry Primary School, Goole

The World Of Books

The world of books,
Books fill your mind with images as beautiful as daisies.
Books help you with your learning so you can be as smart as a scientist.

When you read a book it takes you to another world in your mind,
When you read you can have ideas to write your own book.
You snuggle up in a cosy spot and read a book.

Fairy tales are fun,
Adventure books are adventurous.
Historical books have facts about the past.
By the time you finish a book, you get a new one,
The world of books.

Olivia Winskill (9)
Boothferry Primary School, Goole

Wonderverse

W onder into verses
O nly has the finest verses about purses
N ow there are different words
D on't encounter with mysterious animals or there may be herds
E verybody is welcome to come
R eaders always hum
V ery creative people read into the book
E verybody may see the hook of wonder
R ead into it and you will have pets
S easide verses of nets
E veryone is always happy when they read it.

David Ugainis (9)
Boothferry Primary School, Goole

Champions Galore

You're running out of time
Everything depends on this
If you score
You win
If you miss
You lose
Fans trying to put me off
Screaming and whistling
Palmer's letting me take it
Saying, "You got this boss."
The moment of truth...
"Yeah," chant the crowd
I've done it
Then the best part, the trophy lift!
Palmer lifts it, "Yeah!"

Kaiden Broadhead (9)
Boothferry Primary School, Goole

Football

F ootball is as rough as rugby,
O ther sports are as soft as golf,
O ther sports are just right
T he football clubs people have are as big as a rock,
B ut on the other hand, other clubs are as small as a pebble,
A ll the footballs are as bouncy as a trampoline,
L ots of sports include a field,
L ots of players breathe as loudly as a lion.

Rosie Boateng (9)
Boothferry Primary School, Goole

The Wonders Of Space

The sun is bright like a light
Mercury is a deadly, exotic site
Venus feels like a burning light
Earth is where you can fly your kite

Mars is close to asteroids and they like to fight
Jupiter can be seen from Mars, what a sight
Saturn has amazing rings that are bright
Uranus is like a block of freezing-cold ice
Neptune is so windy it can tear your kite.

Manraj Singh Clair
Boothferry Primary School, Goole

The Space Mission

Three
Two
One
Blast-off
Going into space
There's a lot of gravity
The stars look pretty
Just like our Earth
We can see the moon
Maybe it's my doom

Heard there's gravity
And I jump on the moon
And I jump on Mars
It's red and dusty
And crusty
And I jump on Saturn
My mission is done forever.

Natalia Marcinek (9)
Boothferry Primary School, Goole

Space

Space floater
Space eater
Space singer
Space writer
Space model maker
Space ruler
Space teacher
Space festival
Space dancer
Space party
Space bike
Space worker
Space printer
Space painter
Space explorer
Space reader
Space border
Space neighbour
Space family
Space book
Space alien.

Aleeza Ismail (9)
Boothferry Primary School, Goole

Kickboxing

There's nothing like kickboxing,
For getting your anger out.
There's nothing like kickboxing
For becoming flexible.
There's nothing like kickboxing,
For getting a world title.
There's nothing like kickboxing,
For being a champion.
There's nothing like kickboxing,
For being beaten up by your siblings.

Erin wright (9)
Boothferry Primary School, Goole

The Unicorn

Magical painter
Chasing the stars together
Book reader
Powerful strength
Work together
Nice to each other
Playing with wonderful creatures
Learn from mistakes
No envy
Respectful learner
Cupcake eater
Great adventurer
Kind-hearted unicorn
Pretty care taker
Practical speaker
Good friend.

Monica Kakol (9)
Boothferry Primary School, Goole

Apple Vs The Junk Food

The apple rolled out of the basket,
And then it hit,
The steak,
The steak threw the apple out,
He will never do that again,
The apple found a stick with a frozen pear,
It was a hammer,
Creeping behind him,
Was a chocolate bar with an apple peeler,
Crash, bang, thud.
The apple walked away victorious.

Kai Ward (9)
Boothferry Primary School, Goole

My Sharky Kitten

My sharky kitten is called Penelope,
And she is obsessed with me.
Once, I took her to the beach,
I even let her eat a peach.
My cat is so cute and black,
But strangely, when she walks, her paws clack
When she went into the sea,
And started to bark,
My lovely kitten turned into a shark!

Laura Eduardo (9)
Boothferry Primary School, Goole

What Am I?

I am as cuddly as a teddy bear.
I am magical.
I can make wishes.
I am as small as a mouse.
I am as bright as a diamond.
I am as happy as a clown.
I am as hot as a fire.
I smell like a flower!
What am I?

Answer: A magical unicorn.

Kamila Vilora (9)
Boothferry Primary School, Goole

There's Nothing Like Football

There's nothing like football,
Scoring a bicycle kick.

There's nothing like football,
Scoring a free kick.

There's nothing like football,
Saving a power shot.

There's nothing like football,
Scoring a header.

Artjoms Kolosovs (10)
Boothferry Primary School, Goole

Saturn

S pace is beautiful
A mysterious deep void
T he planet Pluto is as small as an ant
U ranus is as blue as the ocean
R oman gods are named after planets
N eptune is as windy as a jet engine.

Alfie Vaughan (10)
Boothferry Primary School, Goole

The Moon

T he fuel is low.
H ello? I think I'm alone.
E lectricity off.

M y oxygen is low.
O h, is this how it ends?
O h well, time to rest.
N ebulas, such a beautiful view.

Brenton Thorpe (10)
Boothferry Primary School, Goole

The Pain Bucket

A man was painting his house,
He fell off a ladder,
And hit his bladder.

Now he's at the hospital,
And he felt a bit little.
Then he realised,
After he theorised,
He'd shrunk down to an ant!

Zak Lewis (10)
Boothferry Primary School, Goole

Who Am I?

I have a nose as sharp as a knife.
I have a head cleaner than a bowl.
I have a personality like Mr Grinch.
I have little yellow Minions.
I am as bald as a bowling ball.
Who am I?

Answer: Gru.

Alice Souza (10)
Boothferry Primary School, Goole

Who Am I?

I am a blue monkey
I have a friend called Random Cat Owner
I wear a red scarf and a badge
With 91 subs
My name starts with a B
I beat Brenton's sub-count
Who am I?

A Bluey 6T (me).

Mason Hutton (9)
Boothferry Primary School, Goole

What Am I?

I am as tall as a giraffe.
I am as white as a cloud.
People call me the biggest one.
I spin like a merry-go-round.
I power up houses with wind like a superhero.
What am I?

A wind turbine.

Oliver Cerins (9)
Boothferry Primary School, Goole

The Secret Store

A man woke up at dawn.
He whooshed to the store.
He was running low on money so he said, "I'm poor."
But then, when he was gonna pay, he fell onto the floor.
When he woke up he was in the war.

Linden Hanlon (9)
Boothferry Primary School, Goole

Simone Biles The Gymnast

Ribbon swayer
Ball bouncer
Beam roller
Vault jumper
Pro cartwheeler
Great trampoliner
Excellent handstander
Funny roller
Split stretcher
Bar swinger
Rope climber.

Mia Evans (10)
Boothferry Primary School, Goole

What Am I?

I am a banana lover,
I am as yellow as a lemon,
I am as funny as my friend's face,
I am as small as a dwarf,
I am as loyal as a Labrador.

Answer: I am a Minion!

Maisie-Jay Cawthorn (10)
Boothferry Primary School, Goole

About Space

S pace is my favourite thing
P luto is beautiful in the dark
A ll planets are surrounding
C ulture all around
E ach planet is beautiful in its own way.

Ellie Purkis (10)
Boothferry Primary School, Goole

What Am I?

I'm a wild predator with fur,
I'm quiet in time, but loud when I purr,
I'm really fast,
And I'm ready to play,
What am I?

Answer: A cheetah.

Emily Bozek (9)
Boothferry Primary School, Goole

What Am I?

I am tall, but not super tall.
I have a bush on my head.
In winter, my leaves fall off.
I can run, but I can't walk.
What am I?

Answer: A running tree.

Laura Norkute (9)
Boothferry Primary School, Goole

What Am I?

I have squares that never last,
Applied to heat, I will melt fast,
If I'm dropped, I make a mess,
I come from something fresh,
What am I?

Chocolate.

Kacper Michalski (10)
Boothferry Primary School, Goole

The Robots

R obots dance all through the night
O ne stands still avoiding the light
B ut the music never stops
O r they get mad
T he party never ends.

Lucas Cunningham (9)
Boothferry Primary School, Goole

What Am I?

I am slow like a turtle,
I am smelly like a wet dog,
I live in jungles,
I sleep all day,
I am brown like chocolate.
What am I?

Answer: A sloth.

Eva Duggan (10)
Boothferry Primary School, Goole

The Footballer

I wear the number ten,
I'm a ball hitter,
I'm a field striker,
Goal scorer,
I'm a professional,
Bus rider,
Won the World Cup,
I am Messi.

Freddie Jarrold (9)
Boothferry Primary School, Goole

Emotions

Anger steaming out of ears
Jumping with joy
Crying with happiness
Shivering with fear
Hiding in a room
Tears dripping down the face
Dancing with a smile.

Liza Volkova (10)
Boothferry Primary School, Goole

Reptile, My Story

Strong grip
Sharp teeth
Dinosaur cousins
Strong as a shark
Good defender
Good in water
What am I?

Answer: I am an alligator.

Jayden Robertson (10)
Boothferry Primary School, Goole

Our Planet

The trees are falling,
The plants are dying,
The icebergs are crying,
The birds are sighing,
The animals are sighing,
I am global warming.

Riley Harrison
Boothferry Primary School, Goole

Who Am I?

I am eighteen,
I play darts
I have won the world championship against Michael van Gerwen.
Who am I?

Answer: Luke Littler.

Charlie Sharp (10)
Boothferry Primary School, Goole

The Vikings

Sword swinger,
Horse rider,
Boat rower,
Village smasher,
Shield breaker,
Monastery raider,
Terror bringer.

Selin Korkmaz (9)
Boothferry Primary School, Goole

Darts

Darts unrougher
Magic thrower
Eighteen years old
Board hitter
Hitter player
Won so many Premier cups.

Harvey
Boothferry Primary School, Goole

Adele

Song writer
Crowd pleaser
Microphone user
Song singer
Lyric reader
Music pleaser.

Mollie-Ann Malcolmson (10)
Boothferry Primary School, Goole

What Am I?

I am cuddly
I am soft as a teddy bear
I am fluffy as a blanket
I am black as charcoal.

Tansy-Rose Fletcher-Rance (9)
Boothferry Primary School, Goole

Ding Dong Nanny And Her Doppelganger

My nanny looks like Val Garland. She's no ordinary nanny. She is a Ding Dong granny!
Ding Dong, my nanny, loves Gaviscon.
My nanny has white pearly teeth, and if you go to the bathroom at night, they will be there floating in a jar next to the sink.
Ding Dong dentures.
Nanny Val does not have normal dogs.
She has rat dogs.
They have itchy, scaly skin and no hair on their backs.
Their teeth are like vampires, and their faces are flat.
Not Ding Dong.
Nanny loves cats and dogs.
But hasn't found her prince.
Even though she's kissed a lot of frogs.
My nanny and Val have Ding Dong's delicious bleached blond hair.
Nanny and Val have marvellous mega glasses, darling.
Which is Ding Dong!
Nanny Val drives a mini, but she doesn't think she's very skinny.
Nanny is like Val, very trendy, but she's not so bendy.

Nanny thinks her dinners are nice, but they're mainly always rice.
Ding Dong Nanny and her doppelganger Val.

Roux Williams (10)
Donington Cowley Endowed Primary School, Donington

Football

Football is a sport where there are eleven players on each team.
Football is not just a sport
It is also to have fun and respect.
Communication in football helps players know what they're doing.
Football has one key player in a team
And it is a captain who leads the team.

Football is full of mixed emotions
Winners are very thrilled
Losers are heartbroken.
The penalties are nerve-wracking.

Football requires a lot of confidence.
Skill and pace energise the game.
The cheers from the fans and coaches hype both the game and the players.
Discipline, respect and passion build a good team.

James Gitau (9)

Donington Cowley Endowed Primary School, Donington

Emotions Of People

The emotions of people, the feelings,
The happiness of people, not about video games
For some people, not about the pains,
But with laughter and banter
The happiness could come from Santa.
Sadness, sometimes sadness could come from
Madness, crying, weeping,
All signs of sadness or in this
Case madness, stormy, angry,
You could storm off with a grey cloud
Over your head.
You could confront someone with threat,
Emotions are powerful.
Some colourful, people have emotions, it's nothing to hide,
But it's something to put inside.

Brooke Conway (10)
Donington Cowley Endowed Primary School, Donington

The Dragon

Once upon a time, there lived a fiery red dragon. He lived far in the woods. No one dared to go in there. He had massive shiny teeth, massive long wings, and flaming hot breath.
One day, suddenly, a man went into the woods. He went far down and saw the dragon. The dragon saw the man. The man was terrified. The dragon went up to the man whilst the man was on the floor.
The dragon lay on the floor, too. Then the man stood up and sat on the dragon. Just then, everyone looked and saw the man having fun. He was riding on the dragon. Everyone then had fun with the dragon, too.

Naderzda Susorova (11)
Donington Cowley Endowed Primary School, Donington

The King Of The Jungle

It has a matted mane, and it is tangled
It has sharp pointy claws like daggers
Its mane is as golden as the grass
It has a fluffy coat like a rug.

In an area of dry grass
With green bright trees
With other animals that are smaller than others
It is searching for other animals.

Powerfully chasing a cheetah for his prey
Like a shooting star in the night sky
The beast is a king devouring his morning breakfast
Searching for a meat feast
Delightedly grasping his prize.

It's a lion.

Nevaeh Webb (10)
Donington Cowley Endowed Primary School, Donington

Wonderful Seasons

Four seasons come together to bring us lots of joy.
First is spring with longer days
Where the animals come out to play.
Second is summer
Where the sun is shining as bright as the deep blue sea.
Then comes autumn
When the leaves drop from the old oak trees
Children play in the big piles made from the leaves.
Winter has now arrived
The snow is falling from the sky.
Children wrapping up warm for the colder days
Days become shorter and night becomes darker
Now it's time for the hot chocolate fun.

Rocco Briggs (10)
Donington Cowley Endowed Primary School, Donington

Minions

These yellow creatures are so mysterious
Who can really take them serious?
They come in all shapes and sizes
But you concentrate on their beady eyes.

Their metal goggles like suction cups on their face
They were on Earth even before the human race.
Waiting for instructions from Master Gru
What is it he will get them to do?

Kevin, Stuart, Dave and Bob
What is going to be their next job?
To save the moon, on to Vector's house in the dark
But beware, they might get eaten by a shark.

Jack Morris (10)
Donington Cowley Endowed Primary School, Donington

My Football Journey

I love to play football
I started playing since age three
I've got so much better since then
Patience was the key

We started as a team
When we were under eight
Winning games and scoring goals
It made me feel great

I like playing football if I'm happy or sad
Conceding goals
And losing games
Really makes me mad

Since I was three, I've improved
Now would you look at me?
I've made lots of new friends
As I carry on with my journey.

Noah Forknall (10)
Donington Cowley Endowed Primary School, Donington

All About Emotions!

E motions are complex
M oving around the world with friends that make you happy
O verjoyed is when you are doing things you love!
T hankful for everyone and everything! Show love!
I maginative means you have imagination! So things are not real
O utstanding means you stand out, you're being yourself!
N eighbourly is where you're friendly and helpful! You're being kind
S upportive means you are with that person every step of the way!

Amaiya Scoot (11)
Donington Cowley Endowed Primary School, Donington

Autumn Leaves

A utumn leaves fall,
U nder the burnt brown was a dark silhouette,
T hough it is cold, autumn is beautiful,
U can play in the crisp, dry leaves,
M any leaves fall,
N o green leaves in sight.

L ots and lots of leaves disappear,
E veryone is playing,
A nd everyone else keeps warm at home,
V ery many people love autumn,
E very leaf you see will be shrivelled,
S o many play, all year round.

Florence Stone (10)
Donington Cowley Endowed Primary School, Donington

It's A Dog's World

We sleep all day,
We play all night,
I creep up at night
And give you a fright.

If I want your food,
I'll lay on the floor,
With puppy dog eyes,
And offer you my paw.

If you shout, think fast
And throw me a ball,
I'll catch it in my mouth
And think I'm 6-foot tall.

I love you forever,
Every month,
Every year,
As long as you let me
Lick your face and slobber on your ear.

Summer Stukins (10)
Donington Cowley Endowed Primary School, Donington

The Night Sky

R each up, try to touch the sky as planets soar by
O h, look over there, there's a twinkling light
C an't you see there's a shooting star, sparkling bright?
K ind stars waving their goodbyes as they disappear in the night
E veryone watching an asteroid go bang as silence spreads around
T ime to say goodnight today as we greet the stars as they shine once again.

Molly Waters (10)
Donington Cowley Endowed Primary School, Donington

Oreo The Fish

O reo is my fish.
R ed is my favourite colour
E lephants are the biggest land animals
O reos are cool.
S nakes are sssuper.

A re crocodiles dangerous?
R hinos are really fast.
E ars are special.

C omputers are sick.
O ctopuses live in the ocean.
O tters are so cute.
L ucky people.

Jenson Archbold (10)
Donington Cowley Endowed Primary School, Donington

Super Spider-Man

His red and blue suit always recognisable
He's always saving people like a real hero
His number of fails is a straight zero
Oh, he is the best superhero
His web-designed outfit
It's so cool, maybe the coolest
I would also say he's the smartest
He swings from building to building
Shooting webs from his hands
And when we see him we say, "Go, Spider-Man!"

Krystal Walden (11)
Donington Cowley Endowed Primary School, Donington

Winter Wonders

There is an avalanche of snow,
I hope it doesn't blow.
The trees are covered in frost,
I hope I'm not lost.

A fire glows
The snow never slows.
Icicles hang from a hut,
And I keep the doors tightly shut.

The water from the river glimmers,
And the ice shimmers.
There is an ice-cold breeze,
And the rivers freeze.

Olivia Gardner (11)
Donington Cowley Endowed Primary School, Donington

My Friends Are Cool And Amazing

Me and my friends have lots of fun
Me and my friends love to play in the sun.
Smiling and laughing is what we do best
Until it's time for a big old rest.
Me and my friends play in the park
Me and my friends have sleepovers when it's dark.
Movies and games, and of course, snacks too
Where would I be without all of you?

Austin Head (10)
Donington Cowley Endowed Primary School, Donington

Winter Ducks

Snowflakes dance in the air,
But no one seems to care.
Little kids come out to play,
While adults go out to enjoy the day.
Two ducks go their separate ways,
And people go out on their sleighs.
Will they meet again,
Don't worry, the bell will ring once more,
Because people knock on their door.

Katy Topliss (11)
Donington Cowley Endowed Primary School, Donington

The Thoughts Within

Thoughts racing,
Never settling.
The thoughts within,
Never coming out.

Hyperfocusing for long times,
The moving to the next obsession.
One thought of making a movie,
One minute later thoughts of a cat.

What a wonder,
With all these verses.
Just to write about,
ADHD.

Felicity Redman (10)
Donington Cowley Endowed Primary School, Donington

My Grandad And Me

Not just my grandad, my best friend too
He works all day
Then at night, I want him to play
Come on Grandad, it's still light
I fetch my football for him to play
Come on Grandad, get in goal
You can save them, you're not old
Well, not to me
You can be quick
You're the best to me.

Ashley Dukes (9)
Donington Cowley Endowed Primary School, Donington

The Circus

The clown isn't even funny,
This ticket cost a lot of money,
The tightrope walker fell
Into a deep, dark well,
They fed the lion different meats
That made people jump out of their seats,
This circus isn't even funny,
Even the magician pulled out a sad-looking bunny.

Tilly Belham (11)
Donington Cowley Endowed Primary School, Donington

My Cat Loki

M y cat Loki,
Y ou're a bit lucky,

'C ause you're my cat, how
A bout that,
T he way you look.

L oki is the name,
O kay, she is a saint,
K itten at ten months old,
I love you.

Rose White (10)
Donington Cowley Endowed Primary School, Donington

Untitled

F ootball is my favourite sport
O ctopus in my favourite animal
O reo is my favourite food
T urtles are so cute
B asketball is a fun sport
A pple is a fruit
L ollipop is a dessert
L ego is a toy.

Tommy Hilton (11)
Donington Cowley Endowed Primary School, Donington

A Beautiful Night!

It's a beautiful night
With the moon shining bright
Surrounded by stars
Hoping you can see Mars
Through a telescope, a girl looks up
A shooting star as bright as a dove
Owls hunting under the moon
Foxes scurrying around in bushes.

Katie Sawdy (10)
Donington Cowley Endowed Primary School, Donington

Egyptian King

S un glimmers over Anfield,
A s the crowd go wild when they see Salah score,
L iverpool are the best, no matter what,
A fter the game, Salah strips his shirt off, whips it into the crowd,
H ome we go with a win.

Charlie English (10)
Donington Cowley Endowed Primary School, Donington

Untitled

F ootball is my favourite sport
O ut on the pitch
O ver the grass I walk
T he whistle blows
B alls are kicked
A nd the fun begins
L egs kick
L ike a tick.

Jack Holmes (10)
Donington Cowley Endowed Primary School, Donington

I Love Football

I love Manchester United
My favourite footballer is Ronaldo
His number is seven
He plays for Portugal
His most famous goal is a bicycle kick
Best footballer is Ronaldo
He has five Ballon d'Ors.

Lexi Reeves (9)
Donington Cowley Endowed Primary School, Donington

Waffle The Cockapoo

W hat an amazing dog.
A brown fluffy dog.
F avourite dog in the world.
F avourite colour ball is green.
L oves his cuddles.
E ven if he's sometimes naughty.

Jasmine Hill (11)
Donington Cowley Endowed Primary School, Donington

The Green Alien

The alien is green.
The alien is tall.
He lives on a planet.
That planet is small.

The planet is red.
The planet is hot.
The alien sleeps on
A fierce, fiery cot.

Charlie Featherstone (9)
Donington Cowley Endowed Primary School, Donington

My Brother

M y brother,
Y ou are great.

B ig brother,
R iley,
O lder,
T aller,
H elpful,
E nergetic,
R eliable.

Spencer Bettinson (10)
Donington Cowley Endowed Primary School, Donington

Untitled

Best class ever,
Falcons are the best,
Better than the best,
We listen and learn,
And we always take turns.
Donnington School has determination,
It makes me happy.

Ella Harris (11)
Donington Cowley Endowed Primary School, Donington

Colours In Nature

T rees as green as avocados.
R oses as red as cherries.
E ggs as white as snow.
E lephants as grey as rocks.
S eas as blue as the sky.

Rosie Lord (10)
Donington Cowley Endowed Primary School, Donington

Kenny

I once had a dog named Kenny,
Who was short and rather smelly,
He had a squashed nose,
And a comical pose,
That looked like he'd run into the telly.

Noah Ward (10)
Donington Cowley Endowed Primary School, Donington

Untitled

F avourite sport
O nside
O ffside
T op sport
B all
A lways playing
L ose
L ose or win.

Dominic Lindley (11)
Donington Cowley Endowed Primary School, Donington

Godzilla

Godzilla is the most strongest lizard in the world, and also the most cool. Abilities like a titanic breath and also spinning his tail.

Harvey Gilbert (9)

Donington Cowley Endowed Primary School, Donington

Do You Feel The Power Of The Gladiators?

There lived a girl called Holly that loved the Gladiators.
Holly never stopped watching Gladiators until she saw an alligator.
Snap! went the alligator with her jaw
Scrape! went the alligator with her claw.
"Ouch, that hurt!" shouted Holly.
In popped her sister Molly who made her jolly.
And now no alligators
Bite the Gladiators.
Which means they can fight like a champ
And run up the ramp.

Lillie Nash (9)
Great Massingham CE Primary School, Great Massingham

The Incident Of The Harvest Spirit

Come close my friend and take a seat
And listen to our harvest tale that you may seek.
Let my friend and I
Tell you about the incident of the harvest spirit.

It was late one autumn night.
While having fun, getting lost in the tall corn maze
I heard a crow squawk
Though it was not a normal sound.
Then it appeared right before me
There it was, the harvest spirit in the form of a
scarecrow.

I slowly edged towards it in a daze
Suddenly, I blanked out the fear.
Opening my eyes, three hours later, the voice of a man,
"Come my great people, bring your scythes and sickles
Bring your horses and carts,
Gather all the crops as the harvest starts."

As more people gathered
The women and children began to sing,
"The work is hard and heavy, by and by

The days are long, let's keep our spirits high with song
Under the harvest moon sky."

This was different, no harvesters or tractors
But horses... reaping by hand?
Everyone was working to bring in the crops from the land?
This is not 2025!
No, my friend, this is 1898, get to work and lend a hand.

After a long day, tired to the bones, the night had finally come
Alone in the cornfield again
The dark scarecrow figure, The Harvest Spirit appeared, staring into my eyes
I fell asleep
Waking up, in a church, there I was!
Colours flickered a pattern across the floor
From the autumn sun shining through the stained glass window
Songs of harvest echoed in my head.

Now we know about harvest time way back then
We will not take it for granted
To remember how things grow.
Now, it may not be as hard as all those years ago

But we give thanks to the farmers
And appreciate those who put the food on our plate.

Hope you enjoyed my tale of the Harvest Spirit.

Finley Bundock (11)
Great Massingham CE Primary School, Great Massingham

A Friendly Fox

I saw a friendly fox, so slim and shy
Dancing in the bright moonlight.
Its creamy tail swishing away
The silver snow from its velvet ears.
Sniffing the cold midnight air with his pointy snout
So he can stalk and pounce on his prey.
Startled, his ears prick up to hear the sound
Of a passing snowy owl.
Fox retreats to his dark den underground
The owl slowly swoops away.

Phoebe Wade (8)
Great Massingham CE Primary School, Great Massingham

We Are Monkeys

We are monkeys,
We are loud screamers,
Banana eaters,
Four-handed creatures.

We live in the dense jungle,
Swinging from vine to vine,
We also eat fruit from time to time.

We can be intimidating,
Banging on our chests,
We normally migrate in ruthless troops,
Love to clean each other's feet,
We are monkeys!

Charlie Burton (9)
Great Massingham CE Primary School, Great Massingham

Waverley On The Waves

W aves crash against the paddle steamer, Waverley
A s she cruises down the Thames.
V ibration from the paddles and engines
E verybody is cheering on deck
R eady for the adventures ahead on board.
L ower the bridge
E verybody off
Y armouth is the next stop!

George Ridgwell (8)
Great Massingham CE Primary School, Great Massingham

My Puppy Luna

M y new puppy
Y es, she is a whippet

P rickly little teeth
U nder my feet
P erfect little paws
P layful and cuddly
Y appy little bark

L ove you so much
U tterly adorable
N ap time again
A lways make me smile.

Alice Hurst (8)
Great Massingham CE Primary School, Great Massingham

Space

I'm in the sky
Smaller than Venus
I'm hotter than a desert
In the middle of summer.
Hundred and forty million miles
Away from Earth
I am reddish, rusty-red.
Close up I look like butterscotch
People say Martians live on me.
What am I?

Answer: I am Mars!

Jenson Darlow (9)
Great Massingham CE Primary School, Great Massingham

Riddle Poem

I walk on ice
I'm black and white
The sun above burning bright
Melts my icy home
I slip and slide
And love to dive
Who am I?
Lost and cold
With nowhere to call my own.

Answer: Penguin.

Freddie Harrison (10)
Great Massingham CE Primary School, Great Massingham

Stars

Stars, oh stars,
The day has finished
It's time to come out to play.
The full moon is bright beside you
Shine your light tonight in the sky.
Hope you come back tomorrow and shine
Shine brighter than ever.

Theo Carlton (9)
Great Massingham CE Primary School, Great Massingham

Untitled

I am rock
Not a planet.
When you look at me
Through a telescope
I am as small as your pet.
Since discovery
I haven't even gone around the sun once yet.
What am I?

Answer: Pluto.

Cabe Gibbs (10)
Great Massingham CE Primary School, Great Massingham

What Am I?

I can grow
I can shrink
I am super strong and fit
I am as rich as a leprechaun at the end of a rainbow
I can fight like a tiger
What am I?

Answer: I am a superhero.

Noah Watson (9)
Great Massingham CE Primary School, Great Massingham

Football

Football,
High kick, scoring,
Commentators at the match,
Shooting, posing, dribbling, referee,
Goal!

Sonny Lyons (9)
Larkrise Primary School, Great Baddow

Football

Kick-off!
Running, jogging,
Tackling, shooting, passing
Sprinting, saving and scoring.
Hard day.

Tommy Anderson (8)
Larkrise Primary School, Great Baddow

Football

Kick-off
Penalty, goal
Long pass, tackle, kick
Goal, beautiful game, skills, long pass
Winner!

Ishaq Choudhury (9)
Larkrise Primary School, Great Baddow

Gaming

Gaming
Fun, chilling, easy,
Entertaining, Roblox,
Entertainable, interesting, common,
Skilful.

Alivia-Rose McCabe (9)
Larkrise Primary School, Great Baddow

Football

Football
Breaking ankles
Kicking, passing, running
Saving, scoring, skilful, tugging
And goal!

Joshua Akotaobi (9)
Larkrise Primary School, Great Baddow

Puppies

Puppies
Cute little things
Barking around the house
Having fun, getting in trouble
My pet.

Paityn Gench (8)
Larkrise Primary School, Great Baddow

Summer

Summer
Warm calming sun
Beaming happy sunshine
Flowers everywhere, shiny hills
Happy day.

Roseanne Buckley (9)
Larkrise Primary School, Great Baddow

Football

Football
Commentators
Shout when a game is on
We nearly scored a goal
I scored a rebound.

Corey Tyrell (8)
Larkrise Primary School, Great Baddow

Birthday

Birthday
Hip hip hooray
I am nine today, yay
Exhausting but fun, come again guys
Happy.

Miriam Rose Joseph (8)
Larkrise Primary School, Great Baddow

Dinosaurs

Raptor
Sharp claws, T-rex
Swishy tail, scary rap
Tyrannosaurus, diplodocus
Sharp teeth.

Amy Williams (8)
Larkrise Primary School, Great Baddow

Football

I like football.
Midfield, shooting, saving.
Goalscorer, Saka, he scores golden.
One-nil.

Kai Brewster (9)
Larkrise Primary School, Great Baddow

Flowers

Flowers bloom
Summer makes the snails come and go.
Summer comes and the birds come
To chirp that makes the flies run like herds.

When summer comes, the veg is in action
Coming up like they were returning from a vacation
When the veg comes up, the bunnies come nibbling
All the carrots that pop up like popcorn dancing.

Flowers are blooming in all colours and shapes
Pink and blue all in the garden
Check for the poppies in the corner
You will be surprised by the colours.
Saturday has come, which means it's time to spring
into action
Pull the weeds that are at our location.
Put in some bulbs because it's in the plan
Go to the summerhouse to see the birds chirping,
eating and drinking
And to read this poem.

Lucy Clare (10)
Llanelwedd Chuch In Wales Primary School, Builth Wells

Drawing Creatively

Sketching in my room,
Calming atmosphere,
I wouldn't rather be anywhere other than here,
I could make a colourful character,
Or a dark, gloomy landscape,
Crimson red, golden yellow,
Or black, white and grey,
Hearing the pencil hitting the paper,
Unlimited creativity,
It gets more enjoyable every hour,
Escaping reality in my own world,
It feels freeing like a bird flying through the sky,
I could also make a mournful picture,
That might make people cry,
I could make a cheerful drawing,
That would make people's moods lift,
I want to make a drawing that will bring people joy,
To bring joy to every woman, man, girl and boy.

Kaja Czaban (11)
Llanelwedd Chuch In Wales Primary School, Builth Wells

The Tired Hound

Outside in the countryside,
Happily playing in the long, tall, wavy grass
A hound runs fast and fast
Speeding with shiny paws, touching the wet, shiny grass.
As the wind blows by
And as the birds sleep on the trees
The dog rests up by a tree and lies.
His loving owner named Jeff
Sees he's out of breath.
He grabs a bowl and towel
And puts some water in the bowl.
The hound feeling slaughtered, goes for the water
After one hour of resting
The hound goes to play with Jeff.
They have an amazing time
And after a while, they both go inside
To rest!

William Hurford (11)
Llanelwedd Chuch In Wales Primary School, Builth Wells

Rugby

Coming out of the tunnel, the crowd cheering my name
The ref picking up the ball
And me kicking off the match.
Todd driving on with the ball and scoring the try
And the ref will never lie.
The ref is terrible
So we started to tear them all
The commentator said how good I played
Dan Biggar and Alun Wyn Jones coming down
To give us a pep talk
Todd in the scrum and me finishing with a drop goal
We had won 41-22 full-time!
We had won the World Cup
And I'm the captain.

Jamie Duggan (9)
Llanelwedd Chuch In Wales Primary School, Builth Wells

My Holiday

Holiday will be cool.
I won't think of school.
The water park's not strict on rules.
The beach will be hot and sunny.
I'll dip my feet in shining water.
Watching the gulls fly round and round.
After that burger and chips.
It tasted so good.
Ice cream.
Then I go to the slides.
Some are big, some are small.
They look super cool.
The pool was shimmering, nice and cold.
Inviting me, I bowled down.
A human wrecking ball.
Holidays are cool!

Edward Williams (11)
Llanelwedd Chuch In Wales Primary School, Builth Wells

The Football Poem

Mbappé
Hit Lamine Yamal
Ripped his kit
Half-time
Fan got burger and wine
No!
Spain scored an own goal
It was number nine!
It poured with rain
We screamed over and over again
Keeper kicks up the field
Took five out by his heels
Spain free kick
Goal! You see
Now it's penalties
Lamine Yamal goes first
Boots it in the stands
Knocked a fan's hot dog,
Mbappé next.
Trips on his studs, goes wide!

Joseph Lydon (9)
Llanelwedd Chuch In Wales Primary School, Builth Wells

Summer Has Come

As spring goes, summer comes
Flowers bloom as rain goes.
Warm weather and cool drinks
Fish, dolphins, bees, all that you can see.
Ice cream, lemons, and a cherry on top
Running on the beach, sand beneath my feet.

Sunsets on the beach
And a special birthday treat.
BBQs in the garden
Holidays with a pool
Time out of school.
As the sun goes
Leaves fall
Autumn's here, what a ball!

Eryn Edwards (9)
Llanelwedd Chuch In Wales Primary School, Builth Wells

Beautiful Nature

We may shut our eyes but we cannot help knowing,
That skies are clear and the grass is growing.

White clouds appear in the sky above us,
Between the great mountains that lie.

Flowers bloom as summer comes,
Leave frost behind and have some fun.

Roses are red, violets are blue,
Sugar is sweet, so are you.

Roses are red, violets are blue,
Flowers are beautiful, so are you.

Robert Maggs (9)
Llanelwedd Chuch In Wales Primary School, Builth Wells

The Royal Welsh Farming

When it's dawning
The sheep are yawning
All snug in the shed
Where they were just fed.
When we were leaving the shed
We all ran up to bed.

When we were up on the Welsh hills
We were collecting all the ewe girls
From the long green grass
And big bubbling bogs
While all the dogs were jumping
On and off the quads.

I love being a Welsh farmer.

Will Wright (10)
Llanelwedd Chuch In Wales Primary School, Builth Wells

Greedy Gecko

Greedy infant gecko swimming through the reeds,
His hulking sapphire eyes looking like tiny beads.

As the swampy, verdant water rippled ahead,
The gecko twirled his miniature head.

Seeking for slugs with his skin camouflage green,
The gecko's nowhere to be seen.

With his circular tongue shooting from his salivating chops,
The slug swivels and flops.

Ted German-Sparrey (11)
Llanelwedd Chuch In Wales Primary School, Builth Wells

Man's Best Friend

A new era has awoken
Man's best friend has come.
This furry beast shall stalk thee
Zooming past your vision.
Its vision is amazing, as is its sense of smell
So don't be afraid.
Its senses are powerful
Nowhere to hide.
This creature's energetic
So don't bother running.
This dirty beast shall get you anyway
And lick your face.

Finlay Griffiths (10)
Llanelwedd Chuch In Wales Primary School, Builth Wells

Farming

Sheep in the shed, and dad drenching them
Kerry rolling the silage again and again.
Finn harvesting the corn
Mum helping the lambs to be born.
So we go to sleep and wake up at dawn
We go to see if there have been any lambs born.
Jamie driving the tractor through the corn
With me beeping the horn.

Todd Davies (9)
Llanelwedd Chuch In Wales Primary School, Builth Wells

Dart Champion

Three darts
Power to the board
Hit one hundred and eighty
On the dot
Littler...
Is he a bot?
Time is running out
He rushes the shot
He misses the throw
Hits a bullseye
One goes low
The other goes high
Well, what do you know?
I love darts!

Freddie Mills (10)
Llanelwedd Chuch In Wales Primary School, Builth Wells

Cats

Cuddly cat purring.
Clawing cat scratching.
Crying cat meowing.
Chubby cat chewing.
Complex cat contemplating.
Cloned cat copied.
Cold cat shivering.
Civil cat charming.
Crazy cat bolting.
Cantering cat prancing.
Chocolate cat... *yum!*

Amelia Davies (10)
Llanelwedd Chuch In Wales Primary School, Builth Wells

The Naughty Dogs

Dogs, dogs everywhere! Too much hair, they don't care.
Bowls, bowls time for lunch, here come the hungry bunch.
Mess, mess everywhere, their dogs don't share.
Food, food everywhere, these dogs never care.
Love care everywhere, this is the one thing dogs share.

Max Nixon (10)
Llanelwedd Chuch In Wales Primary School, Builth Wells

Spring Is Here

Winter has come to an end
The sun blooming on my chest
The pink buds waving on the trees
Lambs leaping in the fields.

Leaves blowing on my feet
The chicks coming to life
While butterflies and bees are flying in the sky
Spring feels so good.

Annie Davies (9)
Llanelwedd Chuch In Wales Primary School, Builth Wells

Mountains

All around me I could see a resting view with a chilly breeze.
Wonders of life, the waterfalls with their falling beauty.
The birds calling upon us.
The grass rolling with the wind.
The sun shining upon us.
You and I in the midst of an eye.

Tommie Eggerton (10)
Llanelwedd Chuch In Wales Primary School, Builth Wells

Space

S tars shine as bright as a light.
P eople pause to take pictures of the planets.
A stronauts helmets as big as the sun.
C lear skies make stars shine brightly.
E xplosions from asteroids scare monsters.

Eddie Lydon (8)
Llanelwedd Chuch In Wales Primary School, Builth Wells

Wonderverse

A ll aliens amaze and adore him
L oves eating sticky jam
I s a very gigantic and tall guy
E ggs for breakfast every day
N ever leaves deep, dark space
S ad when his big best friends leave.

Albert Grace (8)
Llanelwedd Chuch In Wales Primary School, Builth Wells

Alien

A liens are very stinky animals
L ike to eat the moon,
I t is their favourite food in the world
E veryone hates me, I don't know why
N o one to talk to
S aturn is a very good planet.

Louie Price (7)
Llanelwedd Chuch In Wales Primary School, Builth Wells

Aliens

A liens are not kind!
L ove to eat, slobber, and slime.
I t loves to explore the planets.
E vil aliens taking the planets.
N ot pleasant at the table.
S cary and slimy.

Marlie Hendry (7)
Llanelwedd Chuch In Wales Primary School, Builth Wells

Wonderverse - Planets

P luto is small.
L ovely planets.
A steroids zoom into space.
N eptune is pretty.
E arth is beautiful.
T winkling in the sky.
S aturn is amazing to see.

Evie Bufton (8)
Llanelwedd Chuch In Wales Primary School, Builth Wells

Aliens

A s red as a hot burning fire.
L oves nice, juicy blood.
I s always on the lookout!
E ats crunchy bones with slime.
N ewest alien of them all.
S uper-duper strong.

Kobe Sellwood (8)
Llanelwedd Chuch In Wales Primary School, Builth Wells

Alien Wonder

A liens love dirt.
L oves people.
I t hates children.
E ats biscuits like a monkey.
N esting in a cave, be careful.
S ights are amazing to see as an alien.

Freya Humphreys (7)
Llanelwedd Chuch In Wales Primary School, Builth Wells

Untitled

As the horses' hooves go *clippety-clop*
On the cobbled stable yard
The dogs howl at the wind rushing past
Their shelter.
Finally settling to watch horses jump their last round.

Francesca Finlow-Borrowdale (11)
Llanelwedd Chuch In Wales Primary School, Builth Wells

Aliens

A liens are green and gloomy.
L ive in deep, dark space.
I t's not nice.
E ats monsters.
N aughty and mean.
S ad when they leave their homes.

William Davies (8)
Llanelwedd Chuch In Wales Primary School, Builth Wells

Dragon's Den

Inside of his burning cave
There lies a snoozing beast
In his burning bed of fire
Breathing out smoke
On his bedside table sits
A pile of fire-breathing books
Hot stuff!

Daniel Newton (11)
Llanelwedd Chuch In Wales Primary School, Builth Wells

My Football Poem

As Ronaldo stepped up
To the penalty spot
The whole stadium went silent
When he shot the ball
It hit the crossbar
Rebounded in the net
The stadium exploded in noise.

Evan James (10)
Llanelwedd Chuch In Wales Primary School, Builth Wells

Stars

S hining bright.
T winkling like diamonds.
A mazing colour.
R eally glittery.
S hooting across the moon.

Sadie Jones (8)
Llanelwedd Chuch In Wales Primary School, Builth Wells

Stars

S tars are beautiful
T winkling like the moonlight
A mazing to look at
R acing across the sky.

Sophia Cawser (7)
Llanelwedd Chuch In Wales Primary School, Builth Wells

The Moon

The moon is beautiful
Like a shining, gold lion
Like a juicy, round orange
Tastes like cheese.

Jacob Williams (8)
Llanelwedd Chuch In Wales Primary School, Builth Wells

Squishy Taylor And The Baby Sister

Baby is on the changing table, Dad looks flustered.
"Please, Squishy," he asks me, "can you get the baby wipes? They're in the car." Squishy Taylor to the rescue. I turn to get the car keys, ducking out of our front door to pause in the hallway. *Lift or stairs? Which is more fun? Stairs of course.*
I bolt past the other apartments to the stairway, then leap down the steps like a ninja-gazelle. I slow down at the bottom before I get to the garage. It's always been a bit dark and creepy down here.
Our car is at the far end with the other cars from the eleventh floor. That's when I hear a noise, the kind of rustling, scuttling sound of a rat! So I make a bolt for it. I get back and bolt to bed.

Ava Wykes (8)
Newcroft Primary Academy, Shepshed

Friendship, Kindness, Respect

Finding a friend who's upset or sad,
Try not to make them really mad.

Go up to a positive friend,
So you know it isn't the end!

And then when you are a little flame,
Then you will never get the blame.

Finding a friend isn't easy,
But just say, "Can you be a friend please?"

Go and show them lots of respect,
And be popular with friends instead.

When you and your friends stick together,
It feels like your connections are forever!

Madeline Ellis (8)
Newcroft Primary Academy, Shepshed

My Fluffy Pets

Dog
Dogs are great because they're fluffy
And their coat of hair is puffy.
Types of breeds of dogs
Are Labs, Shih-Tzu and Poodle Service dogs.
The food is normally leftovers
And most dogs can't eat chocolate,
Avocadoes and chives.

Hamster
A few facts are...
Sleep during the day,
Fast runners,
Poor eyesight,
Love to dig,
Short life.

Bunny
Live to 8-12 years,
See behind without moving head,
Do a binky when happy
And eat carrots.

Cat
They purr to heal themselves,
Use tails for balance.

Margot Furber (8)
Newcroft Primary Academy, Shepshed

Seasons

Every day in every world,
Something always changes
Well, what could it be?
Well, when the trees are bare
That means it's winter!

When the flowers start to grow
Well, it means it's spring!

When apples and cherries start to grow
Well, that means it's summer!

When leaves are the colour yellow, red and orange
Well, that means it's autumn!

Elisa Tanasa (8)
Newcroft Primary Academy, Shepshed

Changing Seasons

S easons change all the time.
E ach season does different things, like summer makes leaves the colour lime.
A ny season can change someone's day.
S o when it is May, it is spring, that's what everyone does say!
O nly some people dislike a season.
N obody needs to want to change seasons for no reasons.

Evie Potter (8)
Newcroft Primary Academy, Shepshed

The Life Of A Dragon

He lives in his cave,
He is scary but brave,
He has silky purple scales,
Though they slightly get damaged, when it hails.
He breathes out an orange and yellow fire,
Whilst he flies higher and higher,
The town hates him, but he doesn't care,
Though he floods the town with scare,
He hides in his cave,
As he is very brave.

Annie Palmer (9)
Newcroft Primary Academy, Shepshed

Sand Dune Surfing

I would like to boast
That I went to the coast
To sand dune surf for the day
It was a great way to play
Sand got in my hair
Sand got everywhere
Sand got in my underwear
After the laughter
The best way to end my dream
Was to get a humungous ice cream
Slurp, slurp, slurp, yum, yum, and yum.

Isabelle Baddick (8)
Newcroft Primary Academy, Shepshed

Puppies

I have a dog called Regg
He likes to keep us on the edge
He has a friend called Max
Regg helps us pay the tax.

He is one year and three months old
He pretends he's made of gold
He likes to play with toys
He likes to earn coins.

Nancy Smith (8)
Newcroft Primary Academy, Shepshed

The Wonders Of Space

S upernovas can give people a fright
P eople can see because they light up the night
A fter a while, it will become bright,
C omets will fall like rain
E very night, leaving the Earth in pain.

Thomas Barnes (8)
Newcroft Primary Academy, Shepshed

Which Animal Am I?

I'm super cute and slow.
I love to hang from trees.
I'm soft and cuddly.
I'm as slow as a turtle.
I live in the rainforest.
What am I?

Answer: A sloth.

Emily Hamlet (9)
Newcroft Primary Academy, Shepshed

Faces

Faces are blindingly beautiful in all kinds of ways
You might look different some of the days.

Faces are sometimes heartbreakingly sad
Other times they can be gleefully glad.

Some faces scream, or suddenly shout
They may hide secrets or express some doubt.

A face can tell you a person's story
If you can read it in all its glory.

Let your face be your guide
It is amazing, don't let it hide.

Florence Biddulph (9)
Sonning CE Primary School, Sonning

What Are Friends?

What are friends?
They are as firm as a rock,
As fluid as a river and
As free-flowing as the air.

They have
Secrets to keep,
Smiles to share and
School life to compare.

They will
Make you laugh,
Melt your heart and
Motivate and make things fair.

Message from the author: Some friends are good but some friends are bad if you make the wrong choices.

Emilia Belk (8)
Sonning CE Primary School, Sonning

Spring Animals

A bee said to a flea,
"Shall we go to the sea,
Just you and me?"

A sheep leaps over a heap,
Of hay in the spring.

A fox jumped out of a box
Wearing spring socks.

A bunny thought spring was funny,
Because he could eat jam and honey.

A deer celebrated spring,
Standing by a stream,
Waiting for fish to appear.

I love animals.

Evie Harmston (8)
Sonning CE Primary School, Sonning

Rainbows

Red, rubies, poppies, and sweet, sweet strawberries,
Orange, carrots, tangerines and a boiling, blazing fire,
Yellow, daffodils, lemons, and the bright, blinding sun,
Green, grass, limes, and fragrant spearmint leaves,
Blue, bubblegum, skies, and the never-ending ocean,
Purple, blackberries, and midnight nights,
And to end with the most lovely lavender,
Sadly, our rainbow journey is over.

Tilly Bigus (8)
Sonning CE Primary School, Sonning

Life

Life is a dream
Full of memories
Going on adventures
And telling stories.

Life is family
And family is home
With family around
You'll never be alone.

Life is an inspiration
Making friends
Playing games
It is the best time you spend.

Life has its limit
Yes, it may end
But don't worry
Our love, we will lend.

Minahil Ayaz (8)
Sonning CE Primary School, Sonning

The Girl Who Stands Tall

She stands her ground like a warrior,
Fighting for her rights,
Ready for battle,
With grace and fight,
Stands tall like a mountain,
Proud and empowered,
She's as delicate as a flower,
Yet, strikes like a lion,
A bridge of light,
Sometimes she falls into darkness,
Yet like the sun, she'll always rise,
The girl who stands tall.

Ashling Hyland (9)
Sonning CE Primary School, Sonning

A Girl Who Stands Tall

As brave as a soldier
Ready for war
The courage of a lion
Waiting to roar
A heart full of kindness
And love for you
So naughty and funny
What can you do
Her smile is contagious
From ear to ear
She can giggle for days
Best sound to hear
She stands so tall in life
A sight to see
The girl in this poem
Is Lilliana B.

Lilliana-Rose Bastin (8)
Sonning CE Primary School, Sonning

Amazing Autumn!

Frost bringer
Flower killer
Pumpkin grower
Mammal hibernator
Bird migrator
Sun hider
Scarf snuggler
Harvest bringer
Leaf faller
Bonfire lighter
Cloud bringer
Rain dripper
Jumper wearer
Season celebrator
Soup maker
Firework bringer
Summer destroyer
Guy Fawkes exploder.

Gianveer Sangatpreet Singh Sidhu (8)
Sonning CE Primary School, Sonning

Frost

Winter is here, all of the frost is coming
Down in the deep forest, all the branches sparkle like diamonds.
All is quiet.
People say the Queen of Ice paints all of the branches white
When the trees shake, they fall like stardust.
But now it is over, spring is here
No more pearl white frost
No longer quiet.

Abbey Redfern (8)
Sonning CE Primary School, Sonning

Emotions Jobs

I am Joy,
This is Shy,
This is Anger,
This is Sad,
We all work in your head.

So you have feelings,
Give great thanks,
To us up here,
We work all day,
But not night,
Other emotions,
Give you dreams,
And give you feelings in the night.

Izzy Sawyer (8)
Sonning CE Primary School, Sonning

Rainbow

Red is for love
Orange is for energy
Yellow is for joy
Green in for calmness
Blue is for sadness
Purple is for creativity
Pink is for kindness.

Raife Wilkes (9)
Sonning CE Primary School, Sonning

Butterfly

Butterfly, butterfly fly so high
Butterfly, butterfly happy all the time
Butterfly, butterfly reach the sky
Butterfly, butterfly say goodbye.

Minahil Lone (9)
Sonning CE Primary School, Sonning

The Washing Machine

In the night, the laundromat shakes,
Boom! Bang! Bang! Boom!
The washing noise fills the place,
Rash! Rash! Rash!
Houses are packed with wasting bills,
Click! Click! Click!
When no one's awake, I sneak with skills.

Turning, washing, cleaning of clothes,
No breaks for me I suppose.
My shift's almost over, I cannot wait!
As I see the sunshine on my face.

Suddenly, the machine turns off...
My heart races as I turn it back on.
The lights shut down and the place is dark,
Then something behind me sparks up!

Chizoba E Opurum (10)
St Bernadette RC Junior School, Clapham Park

Nauseous Nightmare

Go to sleep
But you better not weep
See the monster just jump and leap
It will work, that's a promise I'm going to keep
When I went to sleep, I hoped for a good dream
Like eating junk food guilt-free
Or hopping to Mercury
But no, I saw monsters
Making me bleed
Just what they need
Force-feeding me
They couldn't leave me be
Terrible sight to see
They ate for free
They were filled with glee
Stung me like a bee
They ate me, head to knee
They were my friends to my end
Horrible dream to see and send
Blood all over the walls
I hope you don't fall
Bounced me like a ball
Looked like a haunted doll

I don't know why, leave my poor soul
Look at me, I brawl
No one can heal
Can't imagine how I feel
My fate here is sealed
My skin was there, they peeled
I was forced to kneel
Gliding me like a wheel
No one believes me on how I feel.

Pawel Kuras (9)
St Bernadette RC Junior School, Clapham Park

The Tree In Seasons

Spring, the tree hums quietly to itself,
A lullaby to the buds,
Bursting with baby leaves,
Its branches ride the winds
And in its new green glory,
The tree begins to sing.

In the summer, the tree stretches in the sun,
It knows the birds that fly,
The beasts that run, climb and jump,
It yawns and digs its roots,
From its heavily loaded branches,
Deep into the still centre,
Of the spinning Earth.

In autumn, the tree shivers in the shortening day,
Its leaves turn gold,
The clouds pass,
The seeds fall,
The tree drops its coins of gold
The days are rich, little spending of leaves.

In winter, old branches ache,
The tree stands naked in storms,
Frozen, bleak and bare,

Deep underground life lies sleeping,
The tree sleeps,
Waiting for the returning sun!

Milan M (10)
St Bernadette RC Junior School, Clapham Park

Halloween

This is the night when witches fly
On their whizzing broomsticks through the wintry sky
Steering up the pathway where the stars are strewn
They stretch skinny fingers to the waking moon.

This is the night when old wives tell
Strange and creepy stories, tales of charm and spell
Peering at the pictures flaming in the fire
They wait for whispers from a ghostly choir.

This is the night when angels go
In and out of the houses, winging in the snow
Clearing out the demons from the countryside
They make it new and ready for Christmastide.

Jeffrey B (9)
St Bernadette RC Junior School, Clapham Park

My Dreadful Fright

Lightning crashes and thunder roars,
Time to sleep, I snooze off,
Going for water, there is no snoring,
I go outside, and the door shuts,
I panic with fright and get dragged away.

On the journey, trees move,
The sun pops up in the dark,
Dragons fly in the sky, clouds fall,
I hate this! I hate this!
I just want to wake up.

My alarm rings, it's 7am,
My dream gave me a real fright,
Eating my breakfast and take a shower,
Brush my teeth and go outside,
But a cloud is on the ground...

Remiel Reid (10)
St Bernadette RC Junior School, Clapham Park

Strangers To Lovers

You have someone to hate,
But you can't trust your fate.
Making eye contact face to face,
Stomach is full of butterflies.

Hanging out together,
Feeling close forever.
Dreaming about him,
Boom! You have a crush.

You think you hate him,
But you realise you love him.
Your heart is ready to race,
You can't tell him face to face.

You start to date,
Get proposed to,
Have kids.
Never start to age,
With your loved one.

Welwitschia (10)
St Bernadette RC Junior School, Clapham Park

My Best Friend Tobby

To the beach we go
Over the slide he jumps
By the beach he runs
Be serious Tobby!
You are my best friend Tobby
Into the water we enter
So calming
More waves appear
You are so chicky Tobby
Boats splash us
Either way we are wet
Splash, splash
To the shower we go
For now we get dried
Run, run Tobby!
In the car we get
Either way he likes to look out from the window
Now we arrive home
Dream happily, Tobby.

Lucciana Q (9)
St Bernadette RC Junior School, Clapham Park

The Boy Who Cried Ghost

Every single night
I start to get a fright
I lock all the doors, windows and blinds
But during the night, I couldn't believe my eyes.

I feel like my mind is playing tricks on me
But when it gets dark, I can finally see
When I get water
I hear creepy laughter.

I lock and lock but I hear a knock
Guess who is there at my door
A scary ghost with eyes like a bloody ocean shore.

Soraiya C (10)
St Bernadette RC Junior School, Clapham Park

Aliens

They are coming to Earth
To take our land
They warm their hands on the hearth
Have knowledge like the back of their hand.
Crash! An alien!

On UFOs
As they crash
Is that their homes?
Landing in puddles. *Splash*!
Crash! An alien!

Now they go in my rocket
Taking my stuff
From my pocket
In a puff and a huff
Back on the moon once more!

Mirabelle R (10)
St Bernadette RC Junior School, Clapham Park

The Beach

Today on the beach
Making sandcastles
And playing in the sea
Taking off flip-flops
Ouch!
I stepped on a rock!

Today is the day
Last day of summer
Getting swimsuits
Off to the water

Now off to the shop
To get a float and
An ice pop!

The waves are crashing
So we are running
Whoosh, whoosh, whoosh.

Hanna G (10)
St Bernadette RC Junior School, Clapham Park

Chaos On A Tuesday

Chaos, chaos there's
Always chaos, I
Don't know what to
Do, it's always blue. Every
Time I try it doesn't
Go right. Help me
Please. Just answer
Me. Time to time
It's like a light
Flashing through the
Screen with its low
Battery. I wonder when
Chaos is over for me
Because now I am getting
Tired of it.

Sharon Munoz Serna (9)
St Bernadette RC Junior School, Clapham Park

Snake

S ome snakes are venomous, but not all are strong.
The king cobra vs the titanoboa, the cobra would
N ot win. But the powerful, venomous, strong, legendary
A naconda vs the titanoboa would win, all the snakes.
They even named the titanoboa
K ing snake of all.
E ven King Kong is not a snake now
S ome snakes are powerful and fast.

Leonardo Marin (9)
St Bernadette RC Junior School, Clapham Park

Life

I just came from a dream,
Where you could become your desire,
No hesitation to full education,
You could be smart, a loner or a fighter.

Whatever you desire,
Wings of a butterfly,
Eyes of a tiger,
Be whatever you want.

Don't be a sloucher,
Albert Einstein,
Queen Elizabeth,
They worked for their desire, so can you.

Hillary A B Otieno (9)
St Bernadette RC Junior School, Clapham Park

Basketball

B ack of the net
A good try is all you need
S core a hoop
K ick the ball? No, it's not football
E ach player will give a shot
T he best player of the week
B ounce the ball and give a shot
A ble to win? Yes I am!
L evel up on the next level
L ive long baskeball!

Sanchez Blake (9)
St Bernadette RC Junior School, Clapham Park

The Goiky Dragon

The Goiky dragon will give you a fright,
Its purple scales shimmer in the light,
Teeth as sharp as a knife,
Be careful it might bite,
Blazing flames from mouth to nose,
Do not threaten it, you've been told,
If it comes to us, chaos will unfold,
It will burn and bite it has no mercy.

Godswill O (9)
St Bernadette RC Junior School, Clapham Park

Summer

The hot weather
Can't wear leather
The weather has spice
So just add ice.

The scorching sun
Ready for fun?
Going to the park
Just don't let it get dark.

Palm trees
That breeze
Summer life
You can go for a sunny hike.

Silva M (9)
St Bernadette RC Junior School, Clapham Park

Trick Or Treat

Halloween is here
Trick or treat
Candy is coming
Yummy, yummy
It's getting dark.

Witches in the dark
Get ready for the time
Trick or treat
You might get a trick
Or maybe a nice treat to eat
It's time for a trick or a treat.

Sofia Oliveira (10)
St Bernadette RC Junior School, Clapham Park

Graceful Horse

Walk, trot, canter and gallop,
Run across the field,
Gracefully cantering through the woods,
Gorgeous flowers on the hill,
Its beautiful mane,
Glistening in the sun,
The shiny hooves,
Galloping on the hill,
As graceful as can be.

Zosia K (9)
St Bernadette RC Junior School, Clapham Park

Lazy Poem

Sitting on the Astro
Eating a taco
Football is coming
Like a cheetah
No point running
Although it's in sight
Having a bad
Night but still reading a
Funny poem but
Still boring at
This point
No point reading.

Noah M (10)
St Bernadette RC Junior School, Clapham Park

Gotta To Go

Gotta to go at night
Gotta to go, gotta to go
Gotta go where?
Where should I go?
To a phone or a house?

I gotta out
Where should, where should
Help, help
I am lost
Oh no, oh no
I want to go, I want to go.

Emma Figueira de Jesus (9)
St Bernadette RC Junior School, Clapham Park

Bye Winter

Cold winter
Snow falling
Build snowmen
Have fun

Throw snowballs at each other
Winter, winter, what a wonderful season

Too bad you're leaving soon
As flowers bloom.

Anastasia A (10)
St Bernadette RC Junior School, Clapham Park

I Dream, I Dream

In my dream
The stars beam.
As I walk with my dog
Over the path and on the grass
Fresh air, playing, full of fun
My dog and I feel the sun.

Matilde Alves
St Bernadette RC Junior School, Clapham Park

Being A Child

Being a child is ever so cool
Like diving into a swimming pool
Or sneaking food at night
While the others have pillow fights.

Getting attention from mum and dad
And being spoilt, but just a tad!
Getting into trouble with your brother
Because he snitched and told your mother
The only time you'll have to work
Is while trying to hide your smirk
Because Dad stubbed his toe on the baby gate.

Stuffing your face with birthday cake
After eating McDonald's as a surprise treat
Watching the fall of snowflakes
Hoping it will settle for a day off school.

You'll never be bored with a playroom of toys
Adored by all and an imagination that's the greatest tool
There's nothing bad about being a child
It's the best time you'll ever have!

Holly McCann (9)
St Patrick's Primary School, Coalisland

The Roller Coaster Of Emotions

Your mind is busy,
Your heart is sore,
Your face is burning,
And tears begin to pour,
This is a feeling we all have had,
This is the feeling of being sad.

Your heart beats fast,
Your body will shiver,
And when you open your mouth,
Your voice has a quiver,
The touch of your forehead feels wet and balmy,
The palms of your hand feel damp and clammy,
You get to a point where you're close to a tear,
This is the feeling of nervousness and fear.

Smiling, laughing, heart is warm,
No more feelings of being forlorn,
Feeling safe, mind is still, everything is such a thrill,
A burst of happiness inside and out,
This is my favourite emotion, no doubt!

Lily Quinn (9)
St Patrick's Primary School, Coalisland

The Oceans Of Our Earth

This poem's inspired by my holiday in Florida, sailing, snorkelling and swimming with the wildlife.

The oceans of our Earth are full of precious lives,
Small fish, big fish, and even birds that dive!
You'll never guess the creatures that live on the reef,
So many species, colours, and sizes, it's beyond belief!

The oceans of our Earth are important to keep clean,
Our rubbish should go in the bin and not be seen.
Turtles caught in plastic, sharks in an old net,
Work on clearing our oceans is not done or over yet.

The oceans of our Earth are here forevermore,
For many years to come, we can still explore.
Let's do our job and protect the sea,
So it's there forever for you and me.

Ara McCann (9)
St Patrick's Primary School, Coalisland

Military Creations

Warships are fascinating
They are frightening.

Sailors are feared
And also cheered.

Cruisers are dangerous
Also famous.

Battleships are deadly
And also really heavy.

Destroyers are fast
They're always the last.

Submarines are strong
Sometimes the missions go wrong.

Carriers are long
But not super strong.

Aircrafts are small
Like a flying metal raft.

Tiny but strong are tanks
Great for flanks.

AA turrets are cool
But they're no fool.

Daniel Harte (8)
St Patrick's Primary School, Coalisland

We Await

In the heart of France, where dreams take place
Disneyland Paris is a magical place.
A gift from dear Santa, wrapped with delight
A family adventure full of joy in the light.
May 2025, the date we await
With laughter and excitement, we surely can't wait.
Parades filled with laughter, as characters sway
With Mickey and Minnie, we will dance through the day.
So here's to the journey of laughter and play
To Disneyland Paris, where dreams come our way
A present from Santa, a treasure we share
In the Magical Kingdom, love fills the air.

Aoibhe Toner (8)
St Patrick's Primary School, Coalisland

Winter

As winter comes along,
The leaves fall and fall,
Until they're completely bare,
And sometimes not even there.

Snow comes and comes,
It's freezing outside,
The fire is lit,
Animals go to hibernate.

It rains and it rains,
The weather gets worse,
Storms are here,
Thunder is near.

February is better,
But still hats and coats,
The sun peeks through,
Giving a glimmer of hope.

Finally, March nears,
The daffodils appear,
Winter is over,
A new season is here.

Evie-Grace Gates (9)
St Patrick's Primary School, Coalisland

A Note From The Titanic

I've just heard the news,
I can't believe it's true,
The first thing I thought of,
Was to write a note to you.

I'm getting on a lifeboat now,
The captain says it's true.
"There's been a crash with an iceberg,
Down by the boiler room,
Now lower all the lifeboats
And let the people through."

And to all those home in Belfast,
Wherever you may be,
Remember the name Titanic,
For it will surely be,
One of the greatest tragedies,
To go down in history.

Pearse O'Neill (10)
St Patrick's Primary School, Coalisland

Windy Days

Twists and twirls, she dances with glee,
Girlish and playful like a summer dream,
She is an artist up in the sky,
But her blustery swirls aren't what they seem.

Whistling winds rattle windows,
Windblown leaves scuttle around,
A whirlwind of chaos sweeps the land,
Tempestuous gales send trees to the ground.

But wise is she, friend of the sailor,
Who meanders over the housetops,
And waves at the sea,
She is the wind and the wind is free.

Eabha Hughes (11)
St Patrick's Primary School, Coalisland

My Granda

My granda is my hero,
He is a wonderful man,
He is super fit and healthy,
And sports a fabulous tan.

He drives to work with a big, wide smile,
Listening to music all the while.
He reads his Kindle and likes to joke,
And always plays tricks on little folk.

When he's thinking, he strokes his beard,
Which I find kind of weird.
I think he's perfect in every way,
But granny says he's getting worse by the day.

Daire Kilpatrick (9)
St Patrick's Primary School, Coalisland

Legoland

I went to Legoland, hip hip hooray,
Me and my parents went to stay,
We went for four whole days,
There were lots of toys for me to play,
It was the best place I'd ever been,
The biggest dragon I had ever seen,
Made out of Lego bricks,
I was so excited, I was nearly sick!
We had a wonderful time exploring the park,
It lit up when it was dark,
I will always remember my first holiday,
It was in Legoland, where I got to stay.

Cathaoir McKee (9)
St Patrick's Primary School, Coalisland

Lost In Winter

Lost in winter
So quiet, so calm
Robins chirp a whisper
Snowflakes dance on my palm.

The blankets of snow are just too deep
I take a breath of nippy air
I see the creatures beginning to sleep
My lungs start to quiver there.

Each flake is a thought that never dies
The wind begins to moan and cry
All my worries have shot up to the sky
And just in a flicker, they say goodbye.

Logan O'neill (11)
St Patrick's Primary School, Coalisland

Best Friends

B e by your side
E very time with joy and pride
S itting around having fun
T hen some tea and a bun.

F orever friends
R ight there for you
I 'll be there for you too
E ven when we fall out
N ever cry, never pout
D ays go by as we get older
S ometimes we realise as we get older, that best friends are all we need.

Mollie Dorman (10)
St Patrick's Primary School, Coalisland

Friends

Friends are fun,
They're by your side,
And when the playing is done,
You can be yourself and never hide.

They play your game.
And you play theirs,
You might even play the same,
In ones, twos, threes, and pairs.

Cheer you up if you're down,
Help you when you're stuck
Make you laugh when you frown,
And if you have a good one, you're in luck!

Niamh Hughes (9)
St Patrick's Primary School, Coalisland

See The Sea Animals

In the ocean, where fish play,
Colourful creatures are as bright as day.

Dolphins hide in cosy caves,
Jellyfish ride in the waves.

The turtles glide so slow,
Where the seagrasses grow.

Octopus hide, so clever and shy,
While colourful fish swim by.

In the icy waters, where penguins slide,
They waddle from side to side.

Rhys Conlan (9)
St Patrick's Primary School, Coalisland

Fabulous Football

F ootball is the greatest sport
O utstanding players take the centre court
O pponents strive for a goal
T he worst strike is the pole
B enches full of eager players
A crowd chanting lots of prayers
"L et my team score."
L et's hear the crowd roar.

Oisín O'Neill (9)
St Patrick's Primary School, Coalisland

Animals

A nimals are so cute,
N o matter if big or small,
I always see them all on my way to school,
M y dog barks all day and night,
A lways giving you a fright,
L aughing as it licks your hand,
S oaring through the air is a bird, always trying to be heard.

Grace Coyle (10)
St Patrick's Primary School, Coalisland

All About Nature

Bushes swishing,
Leaves swirling,
Draughty windows howling
In the wind.

Rain lashing,
Puddles form,
Rainbow breaks through
The cloudy sky.

Sunbeams on the sand,
Sea waves splashing,
Ice cream truck chiming
A sunny day to enjoy.

Maia McKee (10)
St Patrick's Primary School, Coalisland

Colours

Red is molten, hot and fiery,
Blue is cool, wet and airy,
Yellow is sunny, bright and shiny,
Green is leafy, fresh and earthy,
Orange is warm, sweet and zesty,
White is clean, sharp and crunchy,
Black is dark, cold and deadly.

Alfie McClure (9)
St Patrick's Primary School, Coalisland

Dragons

D angerous dragons.
R oaring.
A s fierce as a lion.
G reat sharp teeth.
O h my goodness, they are scary.
N ever steal from a dragon.
S orry Mr Dragon, I will never steal again.

Tom McAtaseney (9)
St Patrick's Primary School, Coalisland

People

Parents shout
Babies scream
But children these days
Just like ice cream
And the park used to be fun
Because parents are shouting
Babies are crying
And the worst bit of all
It's no fun at all!

Eva Coyle (8)
St Patrick's Primary School, Coalisland

Hop Or Hang

Scary panthers growl
Angry lions prowl
Creepy spiders spin
Colourful fish swim
Slow sloths hang
Happy kangaroos boing
Green snails slide
Brown eagles glide
Grey reindeer clop
But... I stop!

Tom Brady (9)
St Patrick's Primary School, Coalisland

All Animals Are Just Right

A cat rolled up in a mat
A cold black rat

A nice old bat
A bold dog

Leaping like a frog
Koalas lying like a log

The tigers will bite
All animals are just right.

Peter Boyle (9)
St Patrick's Primary School, Coalisland

Everybody Has A Name

Everybody has a name
Some are different
Some the same
Some are short
Some are long
None are wrong.
I like my name
It's special to me
It's exactly who
I want to be!

Niamh Quinn (9)
St Patrick's Primary School, Coalisland

YOUNG WRITERS INFORMATION

We hope you have enjoyed reading this book – and that you will continue to in the coming years.

If you're the parent or family member of an enthusiastic poet or story writer, do visit our website **www.youngwriters.co.uk/subscribe** and sign up to receive news, competitions, writing challenges and tips, activities and much, much more! There's lots to keep budding writers motivated!

If you would like to order further copies of this book, or any of our other titles, then please give us a call or order via your online account.

Young Writers
Remus House
Coltsfoot Drive
Peterborough
PE2 9BF
(01733) 890066
info@youngwriters.co.uk

Join in the conversation!
Tips, news, giveaways and much more!

YoungWritersUK **YoungWritersCW**
youngwriterscw **youngwriterscw**

Scan Me!